Bookkeeping Basics for Entrepreneurs

Taking the Mystery Out Of Your Company's Financials

Jessica Fox

Copyright © 2018 by Jessica Fox, Florida Virtual Bookkeeper LLC. All rights are reserved. It is against the law to make copies of this material without securing written permission in advance from Florida Virtual Bookkeeper LLC. No part of this publication may be reproduced, stored in retrieval systems, or transmitted in any form or by any means – including but not limited to electronic, mechanical, photocopying, and recording without prior written permission from Florida Virtual Bookkeeper LLC.

EDUCATIONAL AND INFORMATIONAL PURPOSES ONLY

This book is provided for educational and informational purposes only and does not provide legal, accounting, or other professional advice or service. Use of any information in the book does not create a professional relationship with Jessica Fox or Florida Virtual Bookkeeper LLC. You should not act on the information provided in this product without seeking additional legal, accounting, or other professional counsel.

Published by: Florida Virtual Bookkeeper LLC
Email: jessica@floridavirtualbookkeeper.com
Web: https://floridavirtualbookkeeper.com

ISBN: 9781720084402

Cover graphic from Pixabay used under CC0 Creative Commons license.

Acknowledgements

No book is ever really written by one person. I'd like to thank my clients for showing me that there is a need for this book and giving me the encouragement to write down what I've been telling them.

I had the great fortune of connecting with Chelsea Hoffer who while interviewing me for an unrelated project, she learned about this book and offered to help me proofread and edit it to ensure that it met its goal of being helpful to a non-accountant, I will be forever grateful for your feedback. Thanks to Emily Cyr for the help with formatting.

To my husband and kids, thanks for putting up with me.

Table of Contents

Preface: What You Will Get From This Guide 7

Chapter 1 - What Is Bookkeeping, and Why Is It Important? 8

Chapter 2 - What Does a Bookkeeper Do? 11

Chapter 3 - Accounting Lingo Translated to English 14

Chapter 4 - Key Reports and What They Tell You 20

Chapter 5 - How Do I Know How I'm Doing? 24

Chapter 6 - Accounting Software- They Are Not All The Same 27

Chapter 7 - Now What? How to Get Your Bookkeeping Done Without Going Broke 34

Chapter 8 - How To Setup Your Books Without Pulling Your Hair Out 36

Chapter 9 - Simplify Your Bookkeeping in 6 Steps 39

You Did It! 42

About the Author 43

Preface: What You Will Get From This Guide

Bookkeeping can be intimidating, but it doesn't have to be. Bookkeeping is often seen as a tedious, detail-oriented and time-consuming task, but it is essential and necessary for any business. At Florida Virtual Bookkeeper LLC, I focus on helping small business owners succeed. I have spent many years helping small businesses like yours with smart, integrated, cloud-based software that saves time and money, helping you run your business better and freeing you to do ... whatever it is you'd rather be doing.

During those years, I've seen business owners overwhelmed by the concept of bookkeeping and struggling to find resources that are easy to understand.

In this guide, you will get a plain English explanation of what bookkeeping and accounting is. You'll also find tips and instructions that will make it quick and easy to keep your business finances in order.

Chapter 1 - What Is Bookkeeping, and Why Is It Important?

Bookkeeping is the process of keeping financial records for a person or business. Accounting is the process of analyzing and reporting on the financial transactions of a person or an organization.

Easy, right? You're probably yawning, but bookkeeping and accounting are important functions of your business. Keep reading to see why you need bookkeeping, and how it can help you out down the road.

Accurate bookkeeping will help you answer questions such as:

> *What are the start-up costs of my business?*
> *What are my revenue streams?*
> *What is the timing of my financial needs?*
> *What is my game plan for unexpected costs?*
> *What are my short- and long-term financial goals?*
> *Is my business profitable?*

Why do I need to have books for my business?

- **To understand the financial health of your business**

    People are investing in you and you are investing in your business. Whether that money is coming from your family, venture capitalists, or a bank, people have invested in you and your success. To show you are responsibly handling these investments, you need to be able to provide an accurate snapshot of the financial health and value of your business.

- **To file accurate tax returns**

    Accurate and up-to-date bookkeeping will allow you to identify deductions that may otherwise be missed, thus saving you money at tax time.

- **To save you money in the long term**

    Getting your books in order soon after starting your business will help save you massive fees for accounting services later on. Setting up early will also save you the hassle of manually entering transactions or searching for a stray receipt from a business purchase 6 months ago.

- **To help secure additional funding in the future**

    If you have clean, auditable accounting records, you will have an easier time applying for loans and lines of credit. You will also be able to show potential investors how you are progressing financially without spending hours tearing your hair out over spreadsheets.

- **To achieve long-term goals**

    Bookkeeping will provide you the insight you need in order to make informed decisions that will determine the future success of your business. If you are hiding receipts in a shoebox under the desk with the dust bunnies, you will never know how to optimize your spending, or how to cut an expense when necessary.

Chapter 2 - What Does a Bookkeeper Do?

A bookkeeper keeps track of the day to day financial transactions of your business and reconciles your accounts to make sure that all transactions are recorded and balances are accurate. He/she can generate reports from these transactions to give you a financial snapshot of your company.

Do I need an accountant if I have a bookkeeper?

A bookkeeper is not the same as an accountant and is not able to provide you with audits or tax advice. What a bookkeeper can do is save you a lot of time by taking care of the data entry, allocation and reconciliation. He/she can also save you money by performing those tasks at a fraction of what an accountant would charge.

However, there are still times when you may need an accountant's expertise. Don't be afraid to pull in an accountant for the following situations, or any time you feel unsure.

- **Setting up your business**

    At the start, an accountant can help you make some

key business decisions. A pro can provide guidance when you are choosing between setting up as a sole proprietorship, a partnership or corporation. He/she can also help you with the administrative tasks of setting up your business and walk you through your weekly and monthly accounting tasks to stay on track. Many entrepreneurs take peace of mind from some initial one-on-one training.

- **Setting up sales tax**

    One of the most common mistakes new business owners make is not properly assessing and setting up sales taxes for their products. Your accountant can get you set up and ensure that you are charging and tracking the appropriate taxes on your sales and services.

- **Checking up on your accounts**

    As a new business owner, you will stumble across challenges in your business every day. If you come across something in your books you're unsure about, just give your accountant a quick call (instead of ignoring it or panicking about it). .

- **Interpreting financial reports**

    Using accounting software, you'll be able to generate some complex reporting that will allow you to complete your tax filings. These reports provide deep insights in to your business's financial health, and your accountant will be able to dive in and help you make sense of it all.

- **Year-end processes**

    It is beneficial to pull your accountant in at year-end to help you with a few processes you will need to get ready for the new fiscal year. This includes closing out your accounts, depreciating assets and setting some financial benchmarks and goals for the coming year.

- **Tax time**

    Taxes can be intimidating for new business owners and with frequent changes to the tax code, it's hard to keep up. Tax season is a good time to involve your accountant so you can be sure you are filing complete and accurate documents (not to mention getting all of the deductions you are entitled to!). Understand your tax obligations from day one! Check in with your accountant to make sure you're not surprised later.

Chapter 3 - Accounting Lingo Translated to English

Accounting uses terminology that may sound like a foreign language to the average person. Most books on the subject will have a glossary in the back that most people never look at—but knowing the basics of this language is a must for any entrepreneur who wants to take control of their finances and make informed decisions.

This quick glossary of the most common accounting terms will help you understand them and relate them to your business.

Accounting

Think of accounting as a sorting tool for your business transactions that makes sense of your financial data. It is simply a way of seeing how awesome your business is doing (assets!) or if it needs some help (liabilities!). Crunching the numbers may be your worst nightmare, but smart accounting and financial statements actually save you and your business time and headaches. I promise!

Bookkeeping

The process of recording your accounting transactions.

Asset

What you own. Maybe it's cash on hand, equipment or a building; if you own it, then it's an asset! Assets = value, so you want to increase them. "Assets, good. Liabilities, bad." —This is the accountants' mantra. Assets are of direct value to your business and are one way to measure how profitable your business is.

Liability

You don't really want liabilities as a business owner, but every business has them (so we have to deal with them). You have to buy things, owe people, and take risks as a business owner, otherwise how can you function? A liability is owing another company, bank or individual money. Think of liabilities as a credit card bill for your financial accounts if that helps (or motivates you into paying them off!).

Double-Entry Accounting

This is considered "real" accounting, the kind accountants like. Double-entry simply shows how your money can start in one place and end up in another. Movement of money through your accounts is visualized by writing a double-entry transaction.

Let's break it down: if you move money from an asset account (such as your checking account) to buy concert tickets (because concerts are fun), then you're going to debit that account for $20 and credit the relative expense account for $20. You took 20 bucks and gave it to another account—that's all!

Double-entry accounting keeps track of money movements by displaying paired debits and credits relative to where you spend or save. Every transaction affects two sides of your business, your assets and liabilities. Double-entry accounting makes sure each transaction is recorded in two places in order to maintain balance. For example: if you spend $1,000.00 on a laptop for the office, your cash on hand will decrease by $1,000.00, but your assets increase in value by $1,000.00. Balance is key!

Income Statement

The report card for your business. A statement showing the money you get and the money you spend. Your expenses will be subtracted from your income to show how much you have left. You need to make money to spend money and grow your business, so find what it is your company does best, develop it, and sell it!

Expense

Money you pay out. Expenses decrease the value of your accounts and equity. Nobody is a huge fan of expenses! You incur expenses when purchasing products or services from another vendor. For example, buying office supplies. The idea is to pay off your expenses (and keep them to a minimum in the first place) so an expense doesn't turn into a liability (which is bad!).

Debit

Debits appear on the left side of your General Ledger, and must always be balanced by credits. Debits are great for increasing your assets and decreasing liabilities, but not so great when they increase your expenses and decrease your income. In short, you can make debits your friend by applying them to asset and liability accounts.

Credit

Think of credits as the twin sibling to debits. Credits appear on the right side of your General Ledger. Credits are great for increasing income and decreasing expenses, but not so great when they increase liabilities and decrease assets. Like debits, there are pros and cons to credits, depending on where you move your money.

General Ledger

The one-stop shop for all debits and credits. The general ledger is like a database for your accounts and their debit and credit totals.

Balance Sheet

An executive summary of your financial position—all of the essentials, none of the boring extra details. What you own and owe, as well as your business' value, can be found here.

Fixed Cost

Fixed versus variable costs—what's the difference? Think of a fixed cost as one you must pay, no matter what. Your rent, for example, is a fixed cost; it doesn't vary depending on the number of goods or services produced or sold by your business. It is a separate cost that must be paid—that simple. Fixed costs are also often referred to as "overhead."

Variable Costs

We know that fixed costs stay the same even with changes to the number of goods and services produced by your business. Variable costs mean the opposite—when your company spends money on production, the variable costs vary according to quantities produced. For example, if you manufacture clothing then the fabric would be a variable cost; as you manufacture more clothing, you have to purchase more fabric.

Equity

The value of your business. If you're the owner of your business, then you have rights to the assets of that business (boss status). As an owner, you of course want the value of your business to increase. Equity increase = right to assets increase. Basically, the more your business is worth, the more value or equity you have. Assets – liabilities = equity, so ample assets with few liabilities is the ideal.

Accounts Payable

What you owe but haven't paid yet. If you haven't paid that utility bill yet, it's in your accounts payable.

Accounts Receivable

What you billed your customers but haven't received payment for yet. If you want to know how much money is owed to you, you'll want to look at your accounts receivable.

Cash Basis

A method of recording transactions only when money is received or paid. If money hasn't changed hands, it doesn't count. This method does not recognize accounts payable and receivable. Many small businesses choose this method because it's easy to maintain and your income isn't taxed until it's in the bank.

Accrual Basis

A method of recording transactions when the income is earned even if you haven't been paid yet. Expenses are recorded when you receive a bill, even if you haven't paid it yet. This is the most common method used by businesses because it gives a realistic idea of income and expenses over time, but it's strongly encouraged that you to monitor your cash flow if using this method to avoid being profitable on paper but with an empty bank account. If your business keeps inventory, the IRS requires you to use this method.

Chapter 4 - Key Reports and What They Tell You

Reports help you gain insight into the financial health of your business. Learning how to understand reports and what they tell you can be intimidating, but don't worry! Below you will find a user-friendly guide to some key reports that will help you understand your finances.

The actual name of the report may change depending on which accounting software you are using, but the end result is the same.

Balance Sheet

Think of the balance sheet as a memo for your investors or for other companies and financial institutions to see how your business is doing. Refer to your assets to see how much your company owns. Under liabilities, you'll see how much your business owes. To view your business' earnings, always refer to equity. The overall value of your business is represented by the balance sheet report.

Account Transactions

This directory for your transactions is searchable by account or date in whatever software you use for bookkeeping. By searching under specific accounts, you can generate a report of that specific account's transactions record.

General Ledger

Check out this report for a complete summary of all your accounts and their debit and credit balances. In this report you can see how much money has come in and out of your accounts. The general ledger is the whole picture, a complete record of your balance sheet, income, and expenses outlining activities across all of your accounts.

Income Statement

This is a report you should be very familiar with. Like, best accounting-report friends. The Income Statement shows you your expenses vs. revenue by simply subtracting expenses from your business' income. It is through this report that you'll know if your business is profitable, and if it isn't. Your Income Statement will also show you where your money is going so you can adjust according. Your revenue, company expenses and cost of goods sold will all be available on the income statement.

Sales Tax Report

The sales tax report will help you understand how much sales tax your company pays and is reimbursed for. Good to know, right?

Income by Customer

This report shows you your business' income from individual customers. Your customer's company name and total payable value (to you and your business) will be visible on this summary chart. This report is a great way to see who your most awesome customers are, and where they're spending their money.

Expense by Vendor

Check this report for separating your business' expense transactions according to the individual vendors (suppliers) you purchase from. Your vendor's company name and total amount paid by your business will show up on this summary chart. This report is a great way to see where you are spending the majority of your money.

Aged Receivables

Go to this report to see where there is money you're waiting to receive, and how long you've been waiting for it. (So you can send a reminder email to those late-payers!) Total aged receivables are tallied and the value appears at the bottom of this report.

Aged Payables

Go to this report to see where there's money you have yet to pay, and how long the payments have been outstanding. This report tracks the aging value of your payables up until you pay them off. (So be a good customer and go pay them!) Total aged payables are tallied and the value appears at the bottom of this report.

Gain/Loss on Foreign Currency

This report shows your gains or losses relevant to the use of any foreign currencies within your transactions. Brief descriptions of the accounts, transactions, transaction exchange rate and average exchange rate on payments are found in columns within the report. This report is used to demonstrate why certain values change according to adjustments in currency. If you don't do business in multiple currencies, this won't apply to you.

Chapter 5 - How Do I Know How I'm Doing?

Here's a list of strong indicators that your business is financially healthy. If you're not able to confidently say say that you're achieving them now, that's ok—now you know where to improve!

You have positive cash flow

The obvious marker of financial stability is money. Now, this is not always a reality for some startups: whether you're bootstrapping, applying for grants or taking investment for corporate equity, you might not be seeing direct revenue from customers yet. Explore all of your avenues for generating revenue, and make sure you know how and when you should be expecting positive cash flow.

You have accurate records

Having a complete and accurate record of transactions is a sign of a professional and prepared business. When you (or your bookkeeper) complete the bookkeeping steps on a regular basis, you will be able to boast organized and accurate financial records. A bookkeeper makes this step easy!

You are paying taxes, loan payments and expenses on time

If you're making payments on time and covering your fixed costs monthly, you are showing financial maturity and responsibility in your business. Creating a financial calendar will help you remind yourself which payments need to be paid when, keeping you on time and organized.

You have an accurate idea of your expenses vs. income

Many small businesses underestimate how much money is realistically required to run their business. It is easy to understand your fixed costs, but your variable costs can add up quickly and are often unexpected. Financially responsible companies factor in extra funds to cover unexpected costs and are thorough when budgeting. Conscious and careful planning will help you decide whether you need to ask for more when applying for a loan, or plan for a larger investment.

You are hitting your targets

As a new small business, you may not be seeing much cash, but you should know how you are progressing in relation to your monthly and yearly goals and targets. You should know your company's unique success markers: Are you signing up customers at the right rate? Are you delivering services as planned? Whatever your targets may be, your next investment will depend on whether you know what the path to success looks like, and how good you are at staying on that path.

You are paying yourself

Small business owners often avoid paying themselves as a way to keep costs down in the business. Paying yourself first, even if it's a modest salary based on what you can afford, is a necessary step to sustaining yourself as a productive owner. Not paying yourself also gives you an unrealistic break-even point. You have to be realistic and honest about your business, and how you are compensating your own time and energy.

Chapter 6 - Accounting Software- They Are Not All The Same

We are long past the age of the old ledger books and manual record keeping. Thanks to technology, accurate recordkeeping of your financial transactions doesn't have to be as tedious and time consuming as in the past. Nowadays there are spreadsheets, desktop software programs, cloud apps and more. There are so many options—how to choose?

There is no one-size-fits-all solution. Here are some things to consider in your research to help you narrow down your choices.

- **Users**

    How many people will need access to create invoices or view reports? Do they need simultaneous access? Are they all in the same location or do they work from different places?

- **Accessibility**

    Do you need access from multiple devices or from your phone while on the go?

- **Features**

    Does your business need more than just basic income and expense tracking? Make sure that the product that you choose offers the features that you need, such as inventory.

- **Customization**

    Depending on your type of business, you may need features beyond a general ledger. Whether you need customized reporting, inventory tracking or point of sale features, make sure that the product that you choose offers them or has an app integration available to add that functionality.

- **Data Backup**

    Choose a tool that allows you to create frequent backups easily, preferably automatically. If you choose a desktop software option, make sure that you have a backup for your backup!

- **Sharing with a CPA or professional bookkeeper**

    Even if you plan to do everything yourself, you never know when you may get stuck or grow enough to need professional help. Select a product that allows for easy access by an accountant and that is supported by a large number of professionals.

- **Automation**

    Time is money. The more features that you can automate, such as importing transactions from the bank so you don't have to manually type them in, the less time you'll spend on your bookkeeping and the more likely you'll be to keep up with it.

- **Frequency of Updates**

    Not all products are made alike. Some have frequent updates to add new features and fix bugs, while others are rarely updated. If you choose a cloud based solution, you will always have the latest version without having to do anything. If you choose other options, you may have to manually install updates or pay a fee to upgrade.

- **Security**

    This is not something to be taken lightly—after all, it's your financial information! If using cloud-based software, be sure that it's a reputable company and check to see what security controls they have in place. If you use a local computer solution such as desktop software or a spreadsheet, you want to make sure that you take precautions to keep that data secure.

- **Pricing**

    Some products are free, some have a flat fee upfront, others have a monthly or yearly cost. While price shouldn't be the only factor in deciding what accounting solution is right for you, it obviously plays a role, especially when your business is still small.

- **Support**

    Some products have 24/7 phone support or live chat while others may only have email support during business hours in the time zone that the company is located in. Consider how you prefer to get help and evaluate the product from that standpoint. Also consider the availability of help documents and tutorials on their website or the availability of a network of certified professionals that you can hire to assist you if you get stuck or need training.

Types of Accounting Software

Desktop Software:

QuickBooks Pro is the most popular option in this category for small businesses but there are others to choose from. This is a good option if your business has a set office location and computer (even if it's just your basement), if you live in an area without reliable internet access and you don't need to do invoicing while on the go.

Pros:

* Pay a one-time fee
* Some automation features

Cons:

* No mobile access
* Limited app integrations
* You have to pay for upgrades
* No access while traveling unless you install it on a secure server

Cloud Based Software and Apps:

This is the fastest growing field of accounting software and for good reason. QuickBooks Online and Xero tend to be the most popular choice for small businesses but there are many other options out there. Cloud based software offers lots of convenience with 24/7 secure access to your data from anywhere you are (as long as you have internet access) and multiple devices.

Pros:

* Available 24/7 anywhere you have internet
* Automatic updates
* Automatic backups
* Lots of 3rd Party apps for added functionality
* Automation features
* Easy access for a bookkeeper or accountant

Cons:

* Requires a monthly subscription
* Requires reliable internet access

Business Software with a "Bookkeeping" Module:

Let's face it, some project management and customer relationship management products may boast a bookkeeping module that may sound enticing because it allows you to have everything in one place for one low price. The features will vary greatly by product but are usually lacking when compared with products designed specifically for business accounting. These may work ok for a service-based sole proprietor but rarely meet the needs of a growing business.

Pros:

* Convenient

* No extra cost if you already use that software for something else
* User friendly (usually)

Cons:
* Very limited features
* Hard to find a bookkeeper or accountant that supports it
* Your business will probably outgrow it

Spreadsheet:

You may think that because your business is new that you can just keep your books in an Excel spreadsheet and this is certainly an option. However, it's important to keep in mind that unless you use a pre-built template with formulas in locked cells, you will need to be careful to avoid errors.

In my experience, I have found that most businesses soon outgrow this. Also, unless you are engaging the services of a professional bookkeeper or CPA to maintain your spreadsheet, a simple error could go undetected for months or years. This doesn't mean that accounting software is error proof, but it tends to be easier to notice with something is off and the reconciliation feature can help you ensure that all transactions are recorded.

In general, spreadsheets don't address a business' accounting needs in an efficient manner. There are better options out there, so I don't recommend a spreadsheet as a long-term solution.

Pros:
* Free

* Customizable if you have a good template or the skills to do it yourself

Cons:

* Difficult to create and maintain
* Subject to errors that could go undetected for a long time if you are not careful
* Limited automation
* Your business will most likely outgrow it

I chose a solution, now what?

Regardless of what option you choose, the most important thing is actually using it.

It doesn't matter how great the program is and how many bells and whistles it has if you go weeks or months without touching it. What was initially a simple task can quickly turn into a big mess that can be hard to figure out.

The next few chapters will walk you through setting up your books. If you do your own bookkeeping, I encourage you to have a professional that is an expert in the software that you chose review your books at least once a year to ensure that there are no workflow errors that can affect your reporting. Doing this before you file your taxes can save you money in overpayments, penalties and avoid the hassle of possibly having to file amended returns.

Chapter 7 - Now What? How to Get Your Bookkeeping Done Without Going Broke

If you don't want to be bothered with the boring day to day stuff and just want to make sure that you are tax ready, hiring a bookkeeper is the way to go.

Most small businesses don't have the means (or space) to hire a full-time bookkeeper as an employee. Not only do you have to worry about their salary and benefits, you also need to consider space and equipment for them to use. This is not feasible for many small business and would be an unnecessarily high overhead cost. You may not have enough work to keep them occupied for even a part time shift, but there is still work to be done.

So how can you get the benefits of a bookkeeper without going broke? This is where a virtual bookkeeper comes in.

A virtual bookkeeper has their own office and equipment and charges you a set rate (either per month or hourly). All of the work is done remotely, taking advantage of the latest technology, so you can focus on growing your business while knowing that the financial details are taken care of.

The costs are usually much lower than putting an employee on your payroll. A part time employee will cost approximately $28,500 per year after factoring in wages, payroll taxes, workers comp insurance, equipment and space costs, etc. On the other hand, a virtual bookkeeper will range in price from $1,200 to $9,600+ per year. These costs are just estimates, the actual amount will depend on a variety of factors including your transaction volume, specific needs (such as tracking inventory), etc. but they give you a pretty good idea to compare your options.

If you are DIY driven or simply don't want to hire a bookkeeper, the next 2 chapters are for you.

Chapter 8 - How To Setup Your Books Without Pulling Your Hair Out

Today, there are plenty of choices for accounting software and they get more user-friendly with each release. Some software is specifically designed for freelancers and business owners, allowing you to DIY your bookkeeping without feeling like you need a college degree for it.

You could do your bookkeeping, daily, weekly, monthly or quarterly depending on the size of your business. For optimal results, I recommend that you do it at least monthly so you can catch any trends while they are still current and avoid having the work pile up. Write it as a to-do on your calendar, since it's easy to procrastinate and next thing you know 6 months have gone by and you don't know where your money went.

Setting up your books can be an overwhelming project, so why not break it down into bite-size pieces? Setting aside 10 minutes per day is a lot easier on your schedule, attention span and stress level. Here is how you can get it done:

7 days of 10-minute tasks to make bookkeeping easy

I actually didn't create this method, but simply enhanced on somebody else's idea. I learned to break down tedious tasks such as these at an entrepreneurial conference years ago. Unfortunately, I didn't write down the name of the presenter or I would be giving credit here.

Monday- Set up your accounting software.

Sign up for the service, edit your business profile, add your business partners (if applicable) as users so they can access your account. Connect your bank account, and categorize 10 transactions to get familiar with weekly tasks.

Tuesday- Customers & Vendors

Categorize 10 more transactions. Now add a customer, enter their data and create an invoice you'd send to that customer. Next add a vendor, enter that company's data, and create a bill you'd send to that service provider. Check out the software's dashboard daily to get a quick snapshot of how your business is doing.

Wednesday- Income

Categorize 10 more transactions. Head to your software's settings and customize your invoice with your company's colors and logo. Create your first invoice and save it as a draft to get familiar with your invoicing feature.

Thursday- Expenses

Categorize 10 more transactions. Now add your first expense account and create an expense quick entry. Take a look at your dashboard, income statement, and expense-by-vendor reports to see where your money is going.

Friday- Making Payments

Categorize 10 more transactions. Then, add a payment to the invoice you created on Tuesday and see how that affects the balances within reports. Next, add a payment to the bill you created on Tuesday and see how that affects your accounts and reports.

Saturday- Accounts & Account balances

Categorize 10 more transactions. Now view your accounts to get familiar with where you've moved transactions over the last 5 days. Make note of which accounts are filed under income, expense, asset, liability, and equity. Check your account balances to see if the debits and credits balance.

Sunday- Payables & Receivables

Categorize 10 more transactions. Then take a look at your receivables report to see any income you're waiting on and from which customers. Next, go to your payables report and look at which vendors you've incurred expenses from and when you owe them payments.

Congratulations, you've just completed a 7-day bookkeeping walk-through!

See? Getting your accounting set up and organized wasn't that hard after all!

Chapter 9 - Simplify Your Bookkeeping in 6 Steps

While bookkeeping can be a lot of work, there are actionable ways to streamline an otherwise demanding task.

With these tips, you can simplify your bookkeeping so you spend less time looking at numbers and more time focusing on growing your business.

1. **Always keep records of all expenses.**

    This is very important for any expenses that may be tax deductible. A shoebox will work in a pinch, but you can take it a step further by keeping your records in electronic format. This means that even if there is a fire or natural disaster, your records are still safe (as long as you backed them up) and you can attach the receipt to the transaction in your accounting software (if your software offers that feature).

2. **Choose a bookkeeping software that fits your needs…. and use it!**

    Any tool is only good if you use it. You took the step to sign up and are probably paying for the software, so make sure that you keep up with it. Just like with the setup, it's easier if you break it up into bite-size pieces. You can break the work up however you'd like—just make sure that you don't let it slide. If you find yourself regularly procrastinating on your bookkeeping, then hiring a professional to do it for you is a good investment.

3. **Use a payroll system.**

   If the business is just you as a sole proprietor, this doesn't apply. If your business is a corporation (or an LLC taxed as one) and/or you have employees, just writing checks as needed and winging it isn't going to cut it. Calculating, tracking and paying payroll taxes is complicated and mistakes can be very costly. There are many affordable payroll services that take this burden and ensures that your business is in compliance.

4. **Keep your personal finances separate.**

   If you don't have one yet, open a business account. There are free options for small businesses, and some banks will allow you to open an account online while in your pajamas—so there are no excuses.

   It's so tempting to pay for your groceries out of your business account. It's your money after all, right? This isn't a good idea as it will add more bookkeeping work for you when it's time to categorize things. Instead, pay yourself first and then buy your groceries with your personal account. It's also tempting to purchase something for your business from your personal account if the business can't afford it at the moment, in this case, transfer funds from your personal account to your business account and then make the purchase.

If your business account is with the same bank as your personal account, you can connect them for instant transfers.

5. **Avoid cash and keep all transactions electronic.**

    Unless you have a brick and mortar store or are selling products at an event or flea market booth, there is no reason to deal with cash in your business. Having electronic transactions makes it easier for you to keep track of things because there is an electronic "paper" trail created for you. No need to worry about tracking Petty Cash, making deposit runs and having to remember to write down what you used the cash for if it didn't make it to the bank.

6. **Develop a weekly bookkeeping schedule.**

    Apart from keeping your memory fresh from doing the tasks regularly, it will also help you avoid mistakes because you won't have to remember more than a week at a time. This practice will give you a warning if something is wrong with your numbers, and it keeps the workload manageable.

    Doing your bookkeeping tasks sporadically and at the last-minute will not only consume a lot of your time, it will make it harder to stay on top of everything.

You Did It!

Congratulations on tackling your bookkeeping!

No matter what stage you are at, you have taken a big step toward having a financially healthy and responsible business. With just a couple of minutes a day, you will save time, money, aggravation, and many frantic late nights.

Keeping your business financially healthy is an ongoing process, so be sure to reach out to a qualified professional if you get stuck!

Wishing you success!

Jessica Fox
Treasure Coast, Florida
https://bookkeepingservice.pro

About the Author

Jessica Fox is an Advanced Certified QuickBooks Online ProAdvisor and Xero-certified advisor that began working in the accounting field in 2001 as corporate bookkeeper. She earned a certificate in Bookkeeping from Miami Dade College in 2002 and worked in corporate accounting as a CFO for a few years before choosing to launch her private bookkeeping practice in order to have the flexibility to work from home while raising her children. She specializes in small service-based businesses and freelancers using QuickBooks Online.

In her spare time, she likes to read, spend time with her family and volunteer. She lives in the Treasure Coast of Florida with her husband and 2 children.

Made in the USA
Coppell, TX
14 August 2023